A Personal Memoir of Overcoming Betrayal

THE CHRISTIAN WOMAN

Suffering in Silence

LYDIA C. STRACHAN

ISBN-13: 978-1-949105-48-3(paperback)

Published by:
Divine Works Publishing
Royal Palm Beach, Florida USA
561-990-BOOK (2665)

DIVINE
WORKS
PUBLISHING
INSPIRE. INFORM. TRANSFORM

www.DivineWorksPublishing.com

CONTENTS

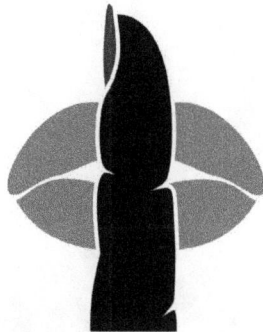

INTRODUCTION

The goal of this book is to help facilitate healing for those who have experienced deep hurt and betrayal and to aid in moving forward with forgiveness in order to have a meaningful relationship with Jesus Christ. This book will also highlight how critical it is to heed to His voice, especially when desiring a relationship or marriage.

To healthily cope on a day-to-day basis, you must know God and learn how to not choose by the flesh. The flesh will desire good looks, fast money, lavish houses and other superficial things; but God desires genuine love, happiness, and peace for his children. The word of God skillfully teaches how one should be treated and how one should treat others. It also fosters true wholeness which comes from God and His agape love.

As you read through the story of my life, you will see how keeping secrets can kill you from the inside out. However, know this, when God has a plan for your life, no matter what the enemy might throw your way, that plan will come to fruition.

The Christian Woman Suffering in Silence.

CHAPTER 1

Contradicting Choices: What Makes us Choose Wrongfully?

Most every little girl wants to be married someday. She dreams of her beautiful bridal dress and her long walk up the aisle. So, what happens when you are all grown up and feel that you are ready because the man of your dreams has entered your life, but everyone around you warns you that he is NOT the one? You feel confident and secure that he is going to love you, take care of you, and treat you like a queen. However, with such opposition how will this work?

Your mother, who you care about so much, advises you to seek prophetic counseling. You are excited to speak with the prophetess because in your mind, she will prove everyone else wrong. It's the day of the meeting and you are on Cloud Nine but are soon deflated as the prophetess says to you that she sees a lot of fighting in the marital house and that your future husband will make you sick. "Sick?" You asked. "How?" And she replies, "with HIV." You being the nice young lady that you are, quickly acknowledge her response with a simple okay and walk out the door with your tail between your legs. However, you consider yourself to be a strong Christian woman and you figure that no matter what, God will heal you and him.

There is a way that seems right to a man,
but its end is the way to death.
Proverbs 14:12 (ESV)

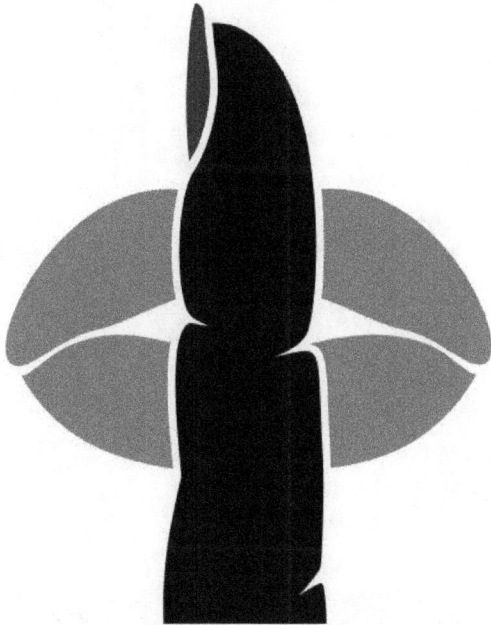

CHAPTER 2

The Engagement: How We Betray Ourselves First

Fast forward a few days later, he gives you the ring right after an argument. Abruptly, he blurts, "I was planning to take you out for dinner and propose on bended knee, now you messed that all up." You are so wrapped up in your own euphoria that you reply with an emphatic "yes," while disregarding the glaring fact this is not the way you envisioned it or how one should be made to feel during a treasured moment such as this. **In essence, you betray your dream for a substandard counterfeit.**

Nonetheless, disregarding that little voice deep within, you start to plan your Big Day. You ask your only friend, the one who you know will support you in anything, to be your maid of honor and she agrees. Somehow, and for a brief moment, everything is alright in your world. The day is here! It's not what you imagined it would be, but it's happening and for that alone, you are happy.

My belief is that everyone needs to be spiritually prepared when it comes to marriage. Why spiritually? Because everything happens spiritually before it manifests naturally. Keeping that in mind, there is a main spirit assigned to target marriages. The spirit of Lilith. This spirit enters a person/marriage through various ways i.e.: generational curses, spiritual sin, sexual abuse, lustful dreams, witchcraft (to control someone against their will), etc.

Prior to exchanging vows, it would benefit one to first perform a spiritual self-check. Something I refer to as "Fix you first"; meaning mentally, emotionally, and spiritually. How does one clear all the baggage? I use a simple 5 step process: 1. Reject, 2. Denounce 3. Disassociate, 4. Repent and 5. Forgive—anything and everything in your life that doesn't line up with the word and will of God.

Before you can love anyone, you must first love God, then yourself, and everyone falls in line afterwards. Loving yourself doesn't mean buying the most expensive things or partying till the sun comes up. It means fully accepting and understanding you first; your likes and dislikes, your beliefs and values, your desires and longings. It requires loving the skin you're in—accepting your differences— knowing that what God says about you is more important than what people, social media, or society says about you. Loving yourself enough to know that no one can complete something God has made so perfectly. Nothing or no one should be able to move you out of what you believe God says about you. Sometimes we need to do a self-check attitude test; meaning, do you walk in the fruits of the spirit? Do you do more of what God likes or dislikes? These self-reflective questions require some deep soul-searching to answer honestly.

Speaking from my own experience, I recognized some of the deeper reasons my marriage suffered spiritually were: generational sins/curses, adultery, fornication, divorce, addiction, and idolatry (serving other Gods), lustful dreams, being wed without God's guidance (allowing someone to put rings on my finger, signing marriage documents other than for the purpose of Holy matrimony), unlawful sex including kissing, holding hands; walking with people from the past or present or even strangers, sexual abuse (being violated/molested as a child), sexual open doors (watching pornography and/or using objects to substitute for a mate).

Could you imagine all this coming from one person's side then marrying someone who had even more spiritual bonadages?

Speaking only from my experience, I carried all of this unresolved spiritual baggage into my marriage. Past hurts, a broken heart, an untamed temper, not knowing God's voice instead allowing other voices/opinions to matter more. We have completely changed the original design of how God intended marriage to be. We've made our own amendments to the manufacturer's design.

The one God has for you fits YOU perfectly!! The two shall become one—equally yoked. A simple meaning of Yoke: *The yoke balances the burden and makes it easier to manage. God is the yoke that keeps the balance in the marriage.* God is a God of order... If God is not first in anything then, whatever it is, it's out of order.

These are a few scriptures which brought light to my situation:

1 Corinthians 11:3 ESV But I want you to understand that the head of every man is Christ, the head of a wife is her husband, and the head of Christ is God.

1 Peter 3:1-4 ESV It's clear that you can marry an unbeliever but by your conversation and how you treat him/her from the (heart) will he/she accept the father. So stop nagging!! Love unconditionally.

1 Corinthians 7:15 ESV But if the unbelieving partner separates, let it be so. In such cases the brother or sister is not enslaved. God has called you to peace so, if they leave you it's okay. Pray, fast, and allow God to work in your marriage. His plans are good and not evil so that you would have an expected end.

1 Peter 3:7 ESV Likewise, husbands, live with your wives in an understanding way, showing honor to the woman as the weaker vessel, since they are heirs with you of the grace of life, so that your prayers may not be hindered. Blessings come through truly loving your wife and vice versa.

1 Corinthians 13:4-8 ESV Love is patient and kind; love does not envy or boast; it is not arrogant or rude. It does not insist on its own way; it is not irritable or resentful; it does not rejoice at wrongdoing, but rejoices with the truth. Love bears all things, believes all things, hopes all things, endures all things. Love never ends. As for prophecies, they will pass away; as for tongues, they will cease; as for knowledge, it will pass away.

Proverbs 6:32 ESV He who commits adultery lacks sense; he who does it destroys himself.

But every man is tempted, when he is
drawn away of his own lust, and enticed.
Then when lust hath conceived,
it bringeth forth sin:
and sin, when it is finished,
bringeth forth death
James 1:14 (KJV)

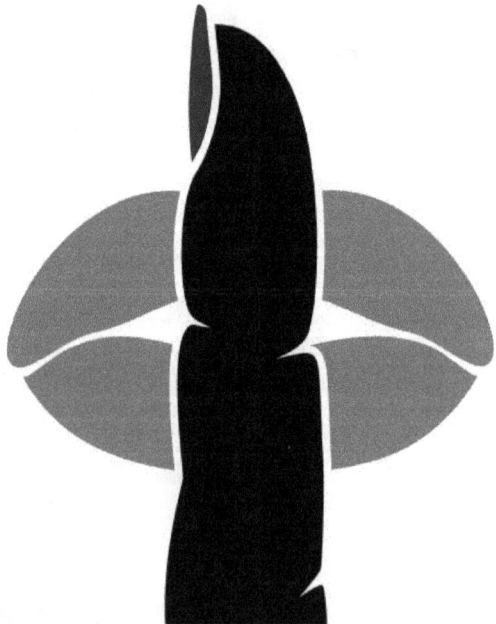

CHAPTER 3

Newlywed Misery: Winning the War of Thoughts

Three months later, you are still in newlywed bliss when one day you receive a call that brings it all crashing down. There is a call from an unidentified lady, she says that your "perfect" husband only married you because she refused him when he asked her using the very same ring he gave her. An irreconcilable sadness fills your heart. You, being spiritually deaf, dumb, and blinded by your own fleshly desires couldn't see this coming. Your little heart is broken, but you can't tell any of your family members or friends because you foolishly assured them that this marriage would work.

You decide to visit your new mother-in-law to seek comfort from her. You pour out your broken heart to her explaining the phone call in detail. Your eyes are red and swollen from crying. But, sadly, this new relative doesn't assist in your healing. In fact, she leaves you in a deeper negative headspace and does not lift the burden as you hoped she would.

The enemy uses these moments of confusion as an opportunity to play with your mind. The very next day I jumped in my car for work and of course the car wouldn't start. I called my husband to see if he could come and get me. The first call no answer, second call no answer and no answer on the third either. I surmise he is with the sweetie and that is why he can't answer his phone. I decide to catch the bus. As I stand at the bus stop one of my co-workers passes by and questions, "hey, why are you walking?" To which I reply, "My car isn't starting." He then chuckles, "You can ride with me if your husband doesn't beat me up." Child please, is all I hear in my head (he is too busy for me). As soon as I hopped in his car, my phone rang; "Hey you trying to reach me?" Of course now he calls, I sourly think while inwardly shaking my head. "Look, the car didn't start so I had to catch a ride." He disapprovingly demands, "A ride with whom?" In disbelief, I respond, " With my coworker, I'll talk to you later."

My coworker smiles and says "Boy, you smell good." The hurt little girl chuckles.

The conversation continues:
At least you're at work on time,
Yeah, I hate being late.
You think your car will be working tomorrow?
Not sure?
Take my number; if you need a ride give me a call.
No problem.

Just like that, the devil uses this one situation to try and break the covenant you've just signed onto.

The phone rings and it is my husband. I ask, "Uh-huh what are you saying?" He responds, "I checked on the car and it's working, I'll pick you up when you get off." "Okay, I'm getting off at six, please be on time."

A few days pass and the car decides to start running hot. I'm unable to make it to the gas station. The calling starts again with no reply. I rummage through my bag looking for my coworker's number and give it a call. Of course he answers on the first ring. "Hey, my car just ran hot. Are you working today?" He replies, "No, I'm off, but I'll come and get you. I am three minutes away, see you in a bit." The enemy doesn't care who he uses to accomplish his dirty work.

Know that the devil is a deceiver; he will try his best to break up anything called marriage. On and on the madness escalates from needing a ride to then "hey, I'm by this nice place getting some lunch would you like any?" To which I reply, "Sure!" After all the calls the mini hero has now become superman.

Everything that's not said and done at home is being done away from home. The tension at home worsens and no one has the other's interest at heart.

Finally, after a few weeks, a seemingly innocent question is posed:

Would you like to go for a ride?
Sure! I'll be ready around seven;
I'll meet you at the gas station.
Okay! Hey, how are you?
I'm good.
You are always on time now....
We both chuckle.

On the ride, you ramble on about what's going on at home. By the end of the night you're dropped off by your car and are met with another not so innocent question, "Before you go, how about I get that good night kiss?"

Your heart leaps because you know kissing another man other than your husband is a total no no. But the enemy won't allow you to feel like it's wrong, he reminds you of what's happening at home. So you agree to only a peck on the cheek. Good mornings and good nights become frequent with lunches in between. God knows all things! No matter how you may try to hide.

As a woman you have to share this with someone, if your friend is someone who will direct you on the right path, thank God, but if you have friends that will support the bad choices, you need to lose them. My friend's fitting advice was, **"How important God is to you? Does this flesh mean that much? Will you lose everything?"**

Another date with this man is set for a meeting. This time the ride ends on the beach and you are about to make a decision that will make you or break you. Here comes the kiss on the lips. Your mind is flooded with conflicting thoughts. Stop. *Stop?* Why? This doesn't feel right. As your desire increases, so do the thoughts about what your husband did, what his mother said and what your Christian friend said. Wait, which one had the strongest facts? As he tries to use soft kisses and light handedly rubs on your legs, you hang your head down in shame. One tear manages to break loose then a few more. "I can't, I just can't. Please take me back to my car". You are met with, "Did I do something wrong?" You reassure him, trying to not hurt his feelings, "No, I just know I need to go. This is not where I should be."

Upon arriving home thoughts storm your mind. What was he thinking? What were you thinking? What was your husband thinking? And more importantly what was God seeing? You're left broken-hearted and feel like a fool.

Sunday comes and you are the first one at church. The sermon should have had your name as it's title. The altar call is given and you decide you can't live this life anymore and change will happen today. You rededicate your life to the Lord and changing is not going back to do the old things that caused you to sin.

The enemy's plan is to steal, kill, and destroy by using all means and at all cost. His best work is done in the mind. **If he could use this one thing to keep reminding you of what you have done, he will be able to defeat you.** There is a quote that cautions us that "a mind is a terrible thing to waste" and that is powerfully true. The Bible says that *"Whatever a man thinks, so is he."* But also, that *no condemnation comes to those that LOVE the LORD.* So now, at this time, having rededicated my life back to Christ and loving the Lord, there is a new feeling in the air. I found all truth flows through you when you have the mind of Christ operating within you.

Note that the enemy could place a thought in your head, but can't read your mind. ONLY God can read your mind because he knows your heart. **When a thought is placed in your mind it's there until you either put it to action or you dismiss it.** With the lack of knowledge and without a full relationship and understanding of God's word the people will perish.

The thief comes only to
steal and kill and destroy;
I have come that they may have life,
and have it to the full.
John 10:10 (NIV)

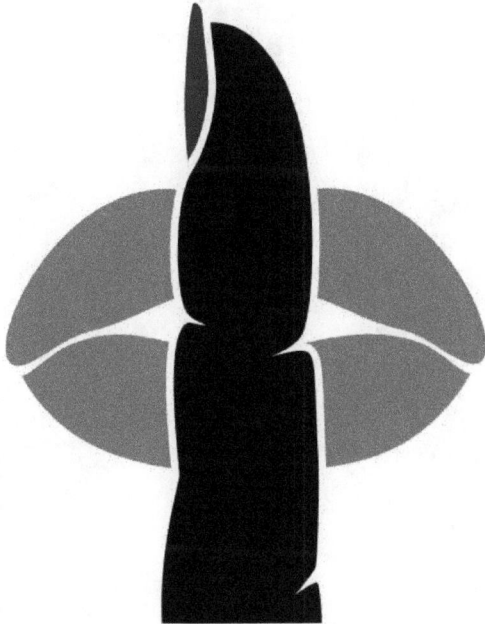

CHAPTER 4

Unwise Decisions: Fools Despise Wisdom and Instruction

So now this thought comes to me: Should you tell him what happened? Yes! Your mind answers, you should. So I ran with my thoughts... Tell him what you did. You question the thought; but nothing happened, I chickened out. If you tell him he will change. This voice in my head was real. That's why you must know your voice from God's voice and the voice of the enemy. If you don't talk to God often enough you wont recognize it. Don't you know your mother's voice, from your father's voice?

I went with the first voice I heard, and allowed that voice to be in control. It continued to speak: "You have to get someone to sit in and listen to this, but who? A pastor? Try this church." The voice was saying who to call, where to set the appointments, everything. Not once had I asked God if this was His will for me. So the voice and I were off on a big quest to get this done. I made the appointment, but now had to convince my husband to show up.

After work I'm home preparing a hot meal trying to be a good wife, while this voice is still in control. As he walks in the door he's greeted with a kiss and hot food. While I'm getting ready for bed I slip in the conversation that I made an appointment at the church and really needed him to be there. The same voice that was in control of my mind urged him, "just go man so she could get off your back for what you did to her." "Yeah, I'll go, when is it?" The date and time are exchanged. At this meeting, I exposed that there was a guy I talked to. I went out with him but nothing happened. The voice said look how brave you were, I know you feel so much better about what you just did. My head swells; I'm feeling proud of myself.

Meanwhile a voice has been whispering in his ear too. He's hearing something telling him she had sex with someone else. How could she? That harlot. This means war!" I left feeling relieved with a smile on my chest while he had anger brewing. This means war!

The Bible says if you don't have wisdom, knowledge, understanding and discernment, ask for it. If not, you will let that voice tell you something again that will cause you to make a decision that will give you a lifetime of hell on earth. Not seeking God on any voice making decisions for you could cost you your life.

Avoiding asking for wisdom, after the war began,

a new voice emerged and spoke saying, "Maybe I should have a baby then he may love me again. Perhaps that is why he is so distant from me. So you plan this all out in your head. Yes, the voice takes control of a new situation. Just like biblical Sarah, you want to get into God's business because you don't want to trust in God and you don't have any patience to wait on God. Get the nice lingerie, soft music, and the perfume and place the plan in motion to make a baby. Weeks later, you call your best friend and tell her that your plan of having a baby worked as you sit on the toilet watching the two lines come up.

You are now lost in the fantasy world of thinking that he will spoil you with your cravings and stay home more with you and prepare the next room for the baby's arrival. However, it is not going the way you planned and now you are pregnant with a baby that's carrying around the spirit of rejection, sadness, and worry, because everything you as the mother feel the baby also feels.

There is hardly any getting up in the middle of the night, asking for weird foods, and getting your feet rubbed because your good husband isn't home. He accompanies you to the doctor a total of zero times during your pregnancy. You are the only married single mother you know. Now we fast forward to the day when you feel those lasting contractions. You try to reach him by phone but to no avail. You are left to call your best friend to take you to the hospital.

Eventually, he is found and arrives at the delivery room after your 16 hours of labor. He enters the room with a fake smile on his face, and no flowers to greet his wife and brand new baby girl. In an effort to keep the peace and keep up appearances, you allow him to place a kiss on your forehead. The first words to come out of his mouth are, "When are you coming home?" It makes your blood boil, but you are left to plaster a smile on showing the good Christian wife you are. Postpartum depression sets in hard and those around you make it no better. You don't even want to see your own baby. As you lay in the hospital bed, your mother in-law and sister in-law arrive to see the baby and bring their negative notions and thoughts with them. They try to find defects in the baby to explain how she could not be related to them. How is it that we tend to do this to other women being a woman yourself, you wonder?

You are now out of the hospital and trying to enjoy your new baby but you cannot because your husband is hounding you to go back to work and to find a nursery for your baby. Your baby has to go to a nursery because none of the grandmothers want to babysit her. Your mother doesn't like your husband and your mother-in-law thinks the baby is too bright to be her grandchild. What the hell is this? Your heart is hurting and you cannot take much more disappointment, but you just smile and place it all in file 13 never to be remembered.

Time passes and she has started to walk and talk. Her first word is Da-Da. Your heart sinks and you think, this man didn't mix one bottle nor get up once during the night, but she says "Da-Da?" Now the spirit of jealousy sets in. However, you remain and continue to play like none of this is happening.

If any of you lacks wisdom, let him ask God, who gives generously to all without reproach, and it will be given him.
James 1:5 (ESV)

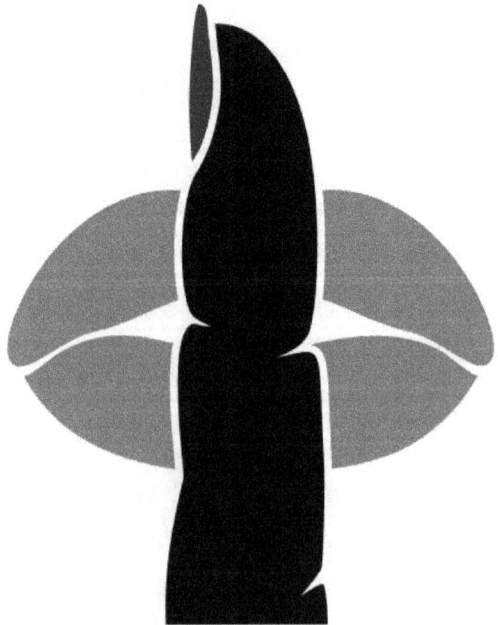

CHAPTER 5

We Suffer in Silence!

One day your "good husband" comes home with two phones. Acting as if you didn't see it, he secures it in his work bag. How could you miss a pink phone? After having dinner and taking a nice hot shower, he falls asleep. You think to yourself, "It's on!" You're tired of all this deceit happening and you have nothing to say. So you decide to wear your big girl panties again and make up your mind that while he's sleeping you are going to check this pink phone.

You now have to prepare your heart and mind because we always feel like we will find something but never decide what will happen when we find it. So you take the phone out of his bag, take it into the bathroom and wrap it into a bath towel so that when you turn it on he doesn't hear it. Your heart and mind is racing because you are not sure what you'll see. You uncover messages, photos, and voice notes. This man is living a life that you know nothing about. Tears start to gather and you are enraged because of what you saw and heard. You storm in the room screaming at the top of your lungs, "you're cheating I knew it!" You awaken him with a hard slap on his head with the phone and he jumps up.

While shouting, you lay out everything you placed in your memory files "13" about the girl who called, what his mother said to you, and what you saw in the phone all at once. In a sad voice, he admits it all and starts to explain that he has the phone because he decided to break it off with her and he took the phone to destroy it. He starts to cry and throws a tantrum. He is sorry that you have to find out this way and promises that it will never happen again. You rant and rave about him leaving the house and his family and you're tired and you want him to go.

But, he holds you in his arms, both of you crying and he says, "That's her plan, if you leave me then she wins. I see it now. I had to go though this just to see what you really mean to me. You're the only woman for me." You could not see it then, but it was his way of mind manipulation. He begins to hit himself in the head and looking at him washed away in tears you feel that this act is genuine. It appears as if he means it and does love you and you believe it's really over between them.

The very next day you wake up, fulfilling your wifely duties as if nothing happened. You walk outside still giving that little church hail to your neighbors as you go off to work, knowing that they are most likely talking about you behind your back. At work, no one knows any information about your life so you can still walk with your head high and act like it's all good. At some point in the day, your nosy coworker calls you and asks that you come to the front because there is a delivery for you. Lost in thought by what it could be, you encounter the biggest bouquet of flowers you have ever seen. Knowing right away who it came from, you suck your teeth in your head but of course that nosey coworker is looking to see your expression so you play it off well. You have to read what the card says for your great co-workers, and it reads "you're the only woman for me and I love you", and you are so happy trying to make it look good for them to see.

As you walk to your office everyone's expressing how "blessed" you are to have a husband like him. The voice in your head is saying, "if you only knew." Meanwhile behind your back, your nosy coworker dismantles your card asking the other ladies why would he say the only woman If they are married? Thanks to that one person who says, "Stop that, they are happily married."

Weeks pass and it seems as if everything is back to normal. He's home on time and you've continued your wifely duties. You all are back to being the happiest family ever. You find yourself sitting in the backyard chilling with a few of your girlfriends, laughing and talking about old time stories. You are happy as can be.

Your phone rings, but the number is not registered so you asked to be excused while you take this call. Upon answering the phone, you hear some women shouting, "Miss you better tell your husband if he ever puts his hand on my niece again, I am coming for him myself." Now this is where the test is, will you turn into the lion you could be or take the "holy" route? Since your friends are so near you decide to go the holy route. "Hi ma'am, I'm not quite sure who your niece is...", but she cuts you off and continues to berate you for your husband. She begins to speak of her own failed marriage woes providing too much information.

As the phone debate winds down to a normal tone, goodbyes are exchanged. You have to now gather yourself quickly while you go back to entertain your friends like that just never happened because you're in a perfect marriage in a perfect world. Here comes the spirit of frustration weighing you down, but you must not show any tension to your friends, so you make up a lie and tell them it's time to go and everyone leaves. Depression and anger now shows up in full force. You are so frustrated that you clean the whole house in an hour.

Then you hear the most horrifying knock at your front door, you jump out of your skin at the first thump. Peering through the window, you see it's the police. Your mind is racing on why they are here? The good Christian wife goes to the door and says, "Good night officers, how may I help?"As you are hoping that the neighbors don't see the police car in your driveway. They are looking for your husband. You tell them that he is not there and wonder if everything is okay. They reply, "Well ma'am it would be best that we speak with him. Please take this number and ask him to give us a call as soon as he arrives."

The officer leaves and you sit at home waiting for him to arrive. As soon as he shows up, you don't allow him to hit the door well before you start to say how some woman called you to say he hit her niece and the police came to see him. And... here we go again, the lies flow like water from a faucet. He starts his plea, "Yes, it happened, but let me explain. She came to my job today to bring me a gift and I asked her if she was crazy for coming here. She explained that if she doesn't have me back in her life she would kill herself. I told her to leave, but she grabbed my shirt. We got into a scuffle and I slapped her. Then she said she was going to the police and my wife would know everything." He said all of that, but the only word you can hear is "everything". You are too busy wondering what everything is. He continues, "Honey, trust me on this one. I don't want to go to jail, I don't want to lose my job. How would I take care of you?" He begins to pack a bag stating that he is going to stay with his mother until it all blows over.

He sets you up with his plan, instructing you to tell the police nothing if they come back. He tells you not to contact him and that he will contact you. It's all happening so fast you don't have time to think or respond. Is he really walking out of the house with a carry-on bag? With a kiss, not knowing if it's the last? The door closes and he's gone. In one breath your husband just told you he will be sleeping at his mother's home because he doesn't want to get locked up and you believe him.

Days go by. You can't sleep because you are too consumed wondering if the police are coming and if he's okay. Years from now, you hope to write a book and laugh at this. Four days later, he is home and he assures you that everything is fine now, and that his police friends cleared things for him. He sees the look on your face and knows you want to ask a few questions. He grabs you in his arms and says, "Please love, I don't want to talk about it, it's over now and we must start our life over."

You assume business as normal. As you walk into work the next day the biggest basket and flowers meet you at the door. You melt at the beautiful mix of roses, gardenias and sunflowers. A tear comes to your eyes, but your coworker thinks that you are overwhelmed. She wouldn't believe the week you just had. Playing it off as normal, your nosy coworker asks you what's on the card. You haven't even looked at it yet. As you slowly turn your back because you don't want them to really see what it says, you read the words, "To our new start" You think, if they really know what's on this card they would figure out something is wrong. So you lie. You tell them it says," I love you forever". You know too, that you will have to ask the Lord for forgiveness.

Fresh from the Pastor's sermon on Sunday, you relish on the fact that finally your house is back to normal. Your husband is home on time, no police knocking on the door and you both are even going out for dinner more often. Oh taste and see that the Lord is good!

However, as a wife, you must be ever ready because life can throw you curve balls when you least expect it. God must be in the midst of your life. Another week or more passes and as you are doing your wifely duties, your cell phone rings. It is another unknown number. It is some strange woman that says, "Your husband has been in a relationship for over a year. I've been in your house before." She continues, "Your curtains are floral and your rug is green." This is the most disrespectful thing you have ever heard but because this conversation fills all the unanswered questions you always had but never got a chance to ask so you let her continue.

Her story gets more interesting as she says, "Your husband and I travel together. We go out together. We rent hotels and enjoy each other. Do you remember that really nice black negligee with the lace on the two sides? I picked it out for you. I told him you would like it. I got one for myself. I'm in love with him." You think to yourself, how in the world this women could be in love with your husband?

THE CHRISTIAN WOMAN SUFFERING IN SILENCE

Trying to still stay strong and saved, you reply, "Ma'am the bible says let marriage be held in honor among all, and let the marriage bed be undefiled, for God will judge the sexually immoral and adulterous." She becomes infuriated and hangs up. However, now you have a full flashback of the conversation in your head thinking of all the things you should have said. He comes into the room and you have this "I'm going to end your life look on your face. He has the audacity to ask you, "What's wrong?" He is about to receive that information. In your full dialect, you answer, "That was your sweetheart. She told me you had her in our house and all the places you both traveled. I'm done, I can't take it anymore. Now I will take care of our daughter and myself. In his most solemn voice, he says, "If you leave me, then she will win. You can't let her win." As you begin to cry, you start to think that he is probably right and you cannot dare let her win. He continues, "You're the only woman for me. I'm done with her. I'm sorry for all the embarrassment, hurt, and sadness I caused. I'm going to do it differently." He says, "God First." This is exactly what you've been waiting to hear. All the fasting and all the prayers have finally paid off. You believe him so quickly just fall back into it all over again.

Sunday comes and he seems so enraptured in service. He even has tears in his eyes during praise and worship and you cannot wait until the altar call. You are so nervous and constantly moving wondering why the pastor's sermon feels extra long today. You wait on the pastor to speak about marriage and how a man should treat his wife, but he does not mention these things today. Altar call came, but this week was not the week. However, it gets better at home. He's reading the Word and asking you questions about different scriptures. He is attending bible study and mid-week worship. Weeks go by and the house is at peace. There are no strange phone calls, no late nights out, more family time, more church and more love. Another Sunday morning arrives and the whole family is dressed alike like a true happy familial unit. At Sunday dinner he looks you in the eye and says "We don't know where death is so we must live daily." Not truly understanding what that meant, you just answer, "Yes, you are right."

Every day you work hard to put all the drama behind you. Revival time at church rolls around and you can see the spiritual smoke from the front door. God's presence really fell in the place as you find yourself on the floor engaging in some good old floor ministry. You know the one you can't find your shoes and your weave is now back and front. You are completely down for the count when the pastor calls for an altar call. As you slowly peel your face from the floor and wipe the tears from your eyes, you notice that your husband is up there with his arms up to the heavens. He has now made the decision you have longed for. "God, I give you all honor and glory for all you have done in our lives. We ask that you

continue to walk with us in Jesus name we pray, Amen",
is your prayer for the night. As you both arise from your
knees and get ready for bed, you think nothing could
be more perfect than life with your faithful husband,
beautiful kids, nice house, nice car, and a great job. This
is what you call happiness as you lay on your husband's
chest and fall straight to sleep.

You are not aware that at the same time in the
spiritual realm, all hell has just broken loose. Time flies
by when life feels great. It's now time for a family vaca-
tion. It's the baby's first plane ride. Everyone is excited.
Days before the flight takes off, he comes home feeling
ill. "What's wrong? Did you hurt yourself?" You ask, "No,
I have a horrible pain in my back," he replies. He decides
to take a shower and take two painkillers and go to bed
refusing to go to the doctor. As you return to the room
with a hot cup of tea for him, he appears to be sleeping so
sweetly, so you ease your way right back out of the room.
During his sleep, you hear him moaning and groaning
with pain only to hear him let out the loudest cry for
pain you have heard in your life. During the wee hours of
the morning he says, "I can't take it anymore more. Take
me to the ER".

Being frightened, you try to stay calm for his sake.
It's a twenty minute drive that feels like two hours. By
the time you all arrive at the Emergency Room, he's in
too much pain to even walk so you have to get assistance
with a wheelchair. His moaning has become so loud that

they decide to take him directly to the physician. The physician advises that your husband take a urine test, blood test, and an x-ray. As you are back and forth from him to running around the hospital trying to get things done, he says, "I feel like I'm going to die." You tell him, "Stop it. Stop it right now. I don't want to hear that. You are a child of GOD. You can't be saying things like that." Rolling him back into the doctor's office, you go back into the waiting room. So many thoughts are running through your head so you start to pray. "Heavenly Father, it's me, Your daughter, I ask for forgiveness of all my sins. I come to you asking for your clarity in this matter. I don't want to be a widow. Why is this happening? What's going on? I need to hear from you Lord, I ask you to show me what I need to do and I ask for your strength while I go through it. I ask that your will be done not my own, in Jesus name, I pray, Amen."

As you sit down with tears forming, the doctor returns to the waiting room asking if he could have a word with you in his office. At this point; depression, fear and worry have taken hold of your mind.

The doctor begins by telling you that your husband's kidneys are failing, but now that he is at the hospital, it can be fixed. Also, he further explains that your husband has an infection which they can give him antibiotics to clear up BUT then the doctor gives you a look that you just cannot understand. You see hurt, worry, and deep concern in his eyes. He continues to say, "what I'm about to tell you may change your life forever, but it depends on you how this will affect both your lives." He starts to explain that there are people that can be assigned to you for counseling and even prayers.

You look at him and begin to cry, "I don't understand what you are saying, please help me doctor." He takes off his glasses and expresses that he is so sorry that he has to tell you this. The doctor proceeds to explain that my husband is diagnosed with HIV and I need to be tested. My happy reality has just taken a turn for the worst. Just then the room goes dark and silent and you are the only one sitting there.....

This was hard for me. I would've never thought that this would happen, but yet, it did. When we receive news like this we always think the worst, never looking at the positive.

Even reading this someone says how can you get positive from this kind of troubling news. I know some people that were diagnosed and died within days because they went into a deep depression because they didn't want anyone to know.

At the end of all this, I have learned the hardest thing to do is face the issue that is also killing people because they just can't or won't do it. It's called forgiveness.

Yes I said it, FORGIVE. No way could I have ever been able to forgive my husband or forgive those women or myself for what they've done to hurt me. They walked, no they stomped, all over my heart and changed my life. There is absolutely no way I could do it within myself without God's help.. Let me share what happened.

When I was writing this book I was in a dry season. I mean dry, no friends, no family, no finances, no love, nothing. It was only me and God. The only thing I did was fast and prayed because I couldn't understand why God was allowing me to suffer. One day I sat in church just in a daze and my apostle for this season in my life said, "Lydia you have to forgive," as he looked me square in my eyes. I was like forgive? BUT YOU DON'T KNOW WHAT HAP-PENED! I heard it again, "Forgive." As I drove home, I grumbled to myself saying that I forgave him already and how was I supposed to forgive if I can't forget because God, You gave me the instruction to write two books about my story. I cried real hard. I even felt like hitting something just like Moses had in his frustration. So, I said "Okay, God what am I supposed to be writing? If you want me to forgive, what's this book all about? In a still small voice he responded with one word, "Forgiveness."

I shed even more tears, because I honestly didn't know how to forgive anymore. I've done it so many times before but this time was different. I needed to first for-give myself then to forgive all others who I felt had let me down. Trying to protect the little pieces of my heart I managed to find, you wanted me to find forgiveness out of it. WOW God, you are full of character. This is now another journey I had to take. I have to first understand the meaning of the word forgiveness then what the bible says about forgiveness. I wasn't ready for what I found, but I learned forgiveness comes in many ways!

By wisdom a house is built,
and by understanding it is established;
by knowledge the rooms are filled
with all precious and pleasant riches.
Mark 11:25 (NIV)

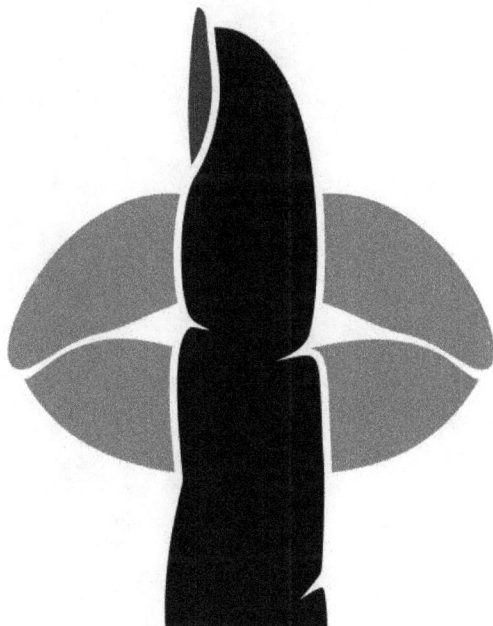

CHAPTER 6

How to Forgive When It Hurts Too Much

Cleanse Your Heart First

Heavenly father, creator of heaven and earth. It's me again, hurt, broken, sad, mad, disappointed, ashamed, bruised, misused, frustrated, tired, stressed, just a mess. I ask you father for forgiveness for all these things that easily beset me. Father remove everything that is not of You... remove all the backbiting, unforgiveness, gossiping, offenses and defenses, lies, regrets, impure thoughts, pride, selfishness, doubt, unbelief, heaviness of heart, free me from negative emotions. Lord, cast it into the sea of forgetfulness. Wash me afresh, and renew a right spirit within me. Cleanse my spirit from all unrighteousness. Thank you father for the new me. Thank you for restoring my soul. As your word says in Psalms 91 allow your angel's to keep charge over me. Thank you for your delivering power. Help me to see others like you do and show them the love only you can give. In Jesus name Amen.

Hurt will come, but be it known that there are ways of dealing with your foes, enemies, adversaries or haters. The bible says pray for them and bless them. This means just how you would go to God for yourself, you should pray for them as well.

For if ye forgive men their trespasses,
your heavenly Father will also forgive you. -
Matthew 6:14 (KJV)

Build Your Relationship with God

Pray: Talk to him as you would anyone else, this is called prayer. Answers are found in his word.

Fast: Start with one hour. That hour is no food, just you and him talking, it's called communication, one talks first, while the other listens then it switches.

Worship: Praise, give him accolades. Tell him what he means to you and how you appreciate what he has done, seen and unseen.

Read the Bible: The Bible says study to show your-self approved unto God. That means to me, that once I have been told anything about God, I check out the information I heard with the Bible. I research it and make sure it lines up with the word of God. Then I ask (God) to explain it fully to me and trust me he answers. I recall

He will even use a spider spinning a web in the corner of my room or an ant trying to take home that crumb you dropped to show you his example.

Action Steps to Forgiveness

1. Forget about it. Let it Go! Give it to God, trust he can handle it better than you ever can.
2. Don't do those things that cause you to remember. Bring each thought into captivity.
3. Stop talking about it. Rehearsing it gives it power over your mind.
4. Keep a positive attitude. Do things that make you genuinely happy.
5. Still show love, especially to all who let you down.
6. Be mature. There is a blessing in not returning evil for evil.
7. Be able to tolerate people (patience) and their perceived shortcomings.
8. Find the positive in your situation. All things work together for the good of them that love the Lord.
9. Make Peace with God and that will give you peace with others.
10. See others as God sees them.

Spiritual Blocks to Forgiveness

Bitterness: Many times people say that they forgive, but forgiveness for them is only from the mouth. The heart and actions say something different.

Resentment: How can I say I forgive when every time your name comes up I recall something negative. You must not remind people about what has happened.

Disappointment: You cannot say i forgive when every time you see that person you try to avoid them or if they call you avoid the call. God sees your face and heart when you meet that person or when that phone is ringing and you don't want to talk to them. No, you can't claim you forgive.

Gossip: You can't be saying negative things about the person or sharing with others personal things they would have shared with you and say you forgive.

Venting: You cannot vent your situation on Social media nor share posts that you know will remind the person or inform others of what they have done. That is not the action of forgiveness.

Witchcraft/Sorcery: You cannot use ungodly means to come into agreement with others against the person you are accusing. You cannot go to a sorcerer and wish death or harm to the person and then say you forgive them.

Show God's Unconditional Love: You cannot say you forgive if you do not show them unconditional love. True forgiveness means if they are hungry, feed them; if they are naked clothed them; visit them if they are in prison.

Pride: You cannot treat people like they are not up to your standard. Acting superior is not forgiveness.

Remain Humble: You cannot speak with anger in your voice and call it forgiveness.

Regret: You cannot ever cause the person to regret being alive because of what they have done.

Lies: You cannot say you forgive if you lie adding to the story to make the story more damaging.

Ask God for forgiveness: Remember, forgiveness is biblical. Only God can enable us to do this, but we must repent and ask for it.

The Importance of Confession

I've heard many teachings, sermons and motivational talks about forgiving yourself... I tried to do this but couldn't seem to find peace with myself until I went into the word of God—which has opened my understanding that we do not have the power to forgive only God has that power. Through Confession we have remission of sin. We can forgive others but have to receive forgiveness from God so that we can have peace. When I finally understood this I went into fasting and prayer and cleansed myself from all unrighteousness.....

The word of God says, *"Whoever conceals his transgressions will not prosper, but he who confesses and forsakes them will obtain mercy"* —Proverbs 28:13

As a believer in Christ you will sin whether in your heart or through the flesh, the father has given us a wonderful thing called the gift of repentance... Everyone doesn't receive this gift but those who have accepted the father have been given this gift.

"My little children, I am writing these things to you so that you may not sin. But if anyone does sin, we have an advocate with the Father Jesus Christ the righteous."
—1 John 2:1

To engage in this scripture it's best to have someone who will be confidential and not judgmental.

"Confess your faults one to another and pray one for another that ye may be HEALED." —James 5:16

"The effectual prayer of a righteous man availeth much." —1 Peter 5:7

After applying his word to my life I felt a heavy burden lifted. I was finally free. Cast all your anxieties on him, because he cares for you.

For if ye forgive men their trespasses, your heavenly Father will also forgive you: Matthew 6:14 (KJV)

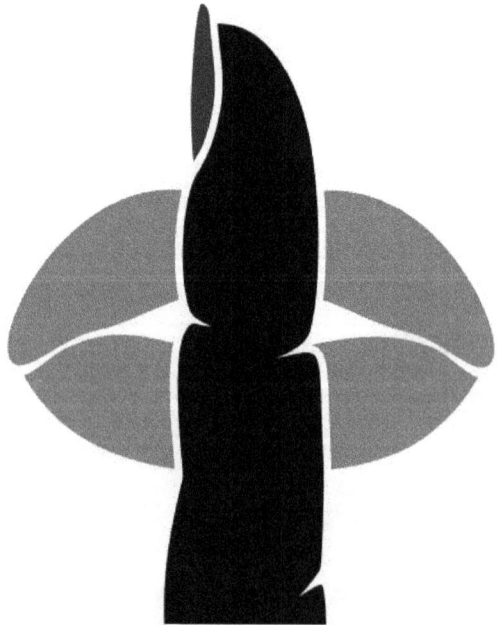

MY PRAYER

Heavenly Father, the creator of heaven and earth. Your word says, in 1John 1:9, that you are faithful and just to forgive us for ALL unrighteousness.

Father, you know the number of hairs on my head and you know the heart of man. Cleanse me with hyssop, purify me with your blood.

Psalms 91 says that you would deliver us from the snare of the fowler. I come before you asking for favor, a sound mind, true salvation, deliverance, wisdom, knowledge, understanding, discernment and the fruits of the spirit for all those that come against me.

Your word says, in Matthew 5:44, But I say unto you, "Love your enemies, bless them that curse you, do good to them that hate you, and pray for them which despitefully use you, and persecute you".

I thank you for their lives, the role they played

in my life, and I ask that your will be done in their lives. I pray that no weapon formed against them should prosper. Allow an open heaven over their lives. I plead the blood of Jesus over them, their families and all you have blessed them with.

Father, I give you thanks for what you're doing in all of our lives. In Jesus name I pray, Amen.

After saying these prayers you should have the peace of God to sleep soundly. Pray and move on with your life with forgiveness in your heart. Continue praying these prayers regularly because it's a process.

Now the Lord of Peace himself gives you
peace always by all means.
The Lord be with you all.
2 Thessalonians 3:16 (KJV)

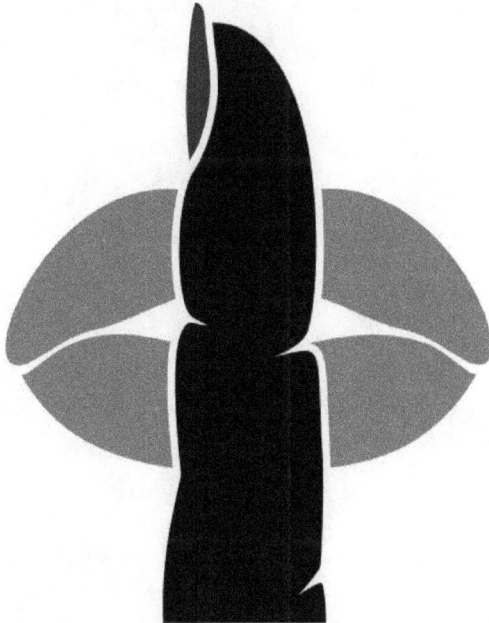

SPECIAL THANKS

I give thanks to the God of Jesus Christ who is the head of my life and to the people that believed and push me when I had no belief in myself.

Also, to everyone who has sown into this book, either by giving funds or by everyday encouragement and prayers to keep me going.

I appreciate each and everyone of you from the bottom of my heart. If I offended anyone, please forgive me. Thank you God for your will being done during this process.

THE END

ABOUT THE AUTHOR

Lydia C. Strachan is an accomplished mother of two, grandmother of one, sister and friend with more than 10 years of experience working in the Hospitality Industry. The R. M. Bailey alumni finds that helping and empowering others provides her with enormous gratification. Lydia's passion is deeply rooted in her faith and love for Christ and her natural ability to be selfless time and again. Having gone through many trials in her life, she seeks continuously to educate those who may be able to acquire a knowledge of how to better maneuver through these tests. Her aim is also to help people find forgiveness in any situation which brings peace and healing through forgiveness. It is no surprise that not only her kids and grandson, but other kids around her gravitate towards her naturally and consider her to be an excellent mother figure in their lives. During her free time, Ms. Lydia spends time studying, finding times of amusement and enjoyment with her family or simply enjoying the best things that life and nature has to offer.

www.ingramcontent.com/pod-product-compliance
Lightning Source LLC
Chambersburg PA
CBHW060258030426
42335CB00014B/1760